The Prayerful Poet

THE PRAYERFUL POET

Found Poems in Hymns of the Past

Beverly Stock

ELM HILL

A Division of
HarperCollins Christian Publishing

www.elmhillbooks.com

© 2020 Beverly Stock

The Prayerful Poet
Found Poems in Hymns of the Past

All rights reserved. No portion of this book may be reproduced, stored in a retrieval system, or transmitted in any form or by any means—electronic, mechanical, photocopy, recording, scanning, or other—except for brief quotations in critical reviews or articles, without the prior written permission of the publisher.

Published in Nashville, Tennessee, by Elm Hill, an imprint of Thomas Nelson. Elm Hill and Thomas Nelson are registered trademarks of HarperCollins Christian Publishing, Inc.

Elm Hill titles may be purchased in bulk for educational, business, fund-raising, or sales promotional use. For information, please e-mail SpecialMarkets@ThomasNelson.com.

Library of Congress Cataloging-in-Publication Data

Library of Congress Control Number: 2020903049

ISBN 978-1-400330805 (Paperback)
ISBN 978-1-400330799 (Hardbound)
ISBN 978-1-400330812 (eBook)

*"To readers, believers, friends and relations,
thanks for your counsel."*

"The Prayerful Poet is a project that pulled at my heartstrings as a secular poet."

-Beverly Stock

Table of Contents

Dedication — v

Epigraph — vii

Part One

A Hateful Eye	2
A Poet's Way	3
Abide with Me	4
All I Ask	5
All In Faith	6
Be Still	7
Beauty of Thy Peace	8
Begotten Faith	9
Children of Dust	10
Children's Rhyme	11
Do Not Wait	12
Eagerly I Sing	13
Epitaph 1	14
Faith in My Heart	15
Faith is My All	16
Faith, My Hope, My Light	17
Gift of Faith	18
Grant Us Peace	19

Heavenly Burden	20
Heavenly Frame	21
His Command	22
Holy Fast and Hunger Sore	23
I Come	24
I Praise and Sing	25
Join To Sing	26
Let Our Joys Be Known	27
Liberty	28
Lift Glories High	29
Loss and Pride	30
Majesty	31
Making Whole	32
Meadows Fair	33
Melodious Sonnet	34
Neither High nor Low	35
O, Hear Us	36
Oblation	37
Practice of Good	38
Rejoice	39
Softly and Tenderly	40
Someday	41
Stand Up	42
Take A Look	43
Take Up Thy Cross	44
Tell The Story	45
Temptations	46
Text of Faith	47
Thankfulness and Praise	48
The Day is Ended	49
The Foundation	50
The Fountain Filled With Blood	51

The Gift	52
Victory	53
What Wonders Wrought	54
When I Wake	55
Ye Faithful	56
Interlude	**58**

Part Two

All Ye	62
Arise	63
Assurance	64
Awake!	65
Below The Skies	66
Best Gift Divine	67
Blessings	68
Bright and Beautiful	69
Church of My Childhood	70
Do Our Best	71
Eternal Gates of Mercy	72
Eternal Love and Life	73
Faith's Hand	74
Find A Voice	75
Funeral Thought	76
Grief and Sadness	77
Guidance	78
Hope and Help	79
How Can It Be?	81
Human Ending	82
I Surrender	83
In The Darkness	84

Just Beyond The River	85
Lost In The Darkness	86
Love Divine	87
Lowly Bed	88
Mercy Broken	89
Mercy Crowned	90
Mercy's Child	91
Mighty Gates	92
Mom	93
My Compass	94
My Vision	95
Mysterious Way	96
On the Wings of the Storm	97
One Holy Passion	98
Praise the Name	99
Straight Race	100
Strength of Faith	101
Strength Within	102
Striving	103
The Joy of The Meek	104
The Poet	105
The Story of You	106
The Test	107
The Voice of Jesus	108
This Is The Time	109
Thou Savior Dear	110
Thy Church	111
Triumph Song	112
Trust And Obey	113
Truth Unchanged	114
Where O Death?	115
Wonders	116
Worship Above	117

Afterword	*119*
Acknowledgements	*121*
Conclusion	*123*
Appendix	*125*
Catalogue Copy	*127*

Part One

A Hateful Eye

On anger's stormy banks I stand,
And cast a hateful eye.
Across the bay, a happy land,
Where once my life I tried.

I was bred with pen in hand,
Words my balm, my faith,
Headed for the promised land,
Penning verse with grace.

Yet chilling winds and poisonous breath,
Did reach my side of shore.
Sickness, sorrow, pain, and threat
I felt and wrote no more.

I yearn to claim that happy place,
I'd be forever blest,
Instead a metal mirror shows,
My twisted face, aghast.

My poem has roots in lyrics from the hymn "On Jordan's Stormy Banks," by Samuel Stennet (1787), which is in the public domain.

A Poet's Way

I am the potter,
Words are the clay.
Phrasing, molding
Verse thy way.
While inspired,
Commotion is stilled.

When weary words,
Seek release,
Soothing rhyme,
Through me speaks.
Joyous words,
Often sway,

The potter just
the voice today.

My poem has roots in lyrics from the hymn "Have Thine Own Way," by author Adelaide A. Pollard (1906), which is in the public domain.

THE PRAYERFUL POET

ABIDE WITH ME

Abide with me,
the darkness deepens,

Swift to its close,
earth's joys grow dim.

Glories pass away,
change and decay.

Faith my guide,
and strength can be.

I fear no foe,
abide with me.

Ills have no weight,
where is death's sting?

Shine through the gloom,
Earth's vain shadows flee,

Abide with me.

My poem has roots in lyrics from the hymn "Abide with Me: Fast Falls the Eventide," author Henry Francis Lyte (1847), which is in the public domain.

… BEVERLY STOCK

All I Ask

All I ask is,
When my heart is pure,
Fill me with life anew,
And mine will then be yours,
To do and to endure,
So I may love the way you love,
So I shall never die,
But live with you the perfect life,
Forever till time is nigh.

My poem has roots in lyrics from the hymn "Breathe on Me, Breath of God," author Edwin Hatch (1878), which is in the public domain.

All In Faith

Hark, the speech of holy voices,
Like the stars in glory stands,
Patriarch and holy prophet,
Holding victory in their hands.

Saintly maiden, godly matron,
Widows who have watched in prayer,
Join in holy concert, singing,
Men of faith, they too are there.

They have come from tribulation,
Washed their robes in holy blood,
And by death to life immortal,
They were born and glorified.

Holy one, the one begotten, light
Of light, blessed he Emmanuel,
Men of faith may we forevermore,
To him give worship and adore.

My poem has roots in lyrics from the hymn, "Hark! The Sound of Holy Voices," author Christopher Wordsworth (1862), which is in the public domain.

BE STILL

Bear patiently the cross of grief or pain,
In every change, the faithful remain.

Be still, my soul: for a heavenly friend
Guides and leads us to the end.

Your hope, your confidence let nothing shake,
Be still, my soul: your faith will undertake.

Future guidance as has shown in the past,
Then all mysteries shall be bright at last.

Be still, my soul: when dearest friends depart,
Then lost love will remain in your heart.

Be still, my soul: the hour is hastening on,
When disappointment, grief and fear are gone.

Be still, my soul: when change and tears are past,
All safe and blessed, we shall meet at last.

My poem has roots in lyrics from the hymn "Be Still My Soul," by author Kathrina von Schlegel, translated by Jane Borthwick (1855), and is in the public domain.

Beauty of Thy Peace

Oh, calm from hills above
In certainty and love,
Drop thy dews of quietness,
Take from our souls the strain and stress,
Bring the beauty of thy peace
Till all our ardent strivings cease.
Breathe through the hearts of our desire
Speak through the earthquake, wind, and fire.
Let sense be dumb, let flesh retire.

My poem has roots in lyrics from the hymn "Dear Lord and Father of Mankind," by John Greenleaf Whittier (1872), which is in the public domain.

Begotten Faith

Of the faith we have begotten,
As the worlds began to be,
Of the things that are and have been,
What the future years shall see.

O ye heights of heaven,
All dominions now to see,
Let no tongue on earth be silent,
Every voice in harmony.

Hymn and chant in thanksgiving,
All unwearied praises be,
Honor, glory, and dominion,
And eternal victory.

My poem has roots in lyrics from the hymn "Of the Father's Love Begotten," which is based on the Latin poem "Corde natus" by author Aurelius Clemens Prudentius (Spain), translated into English by H. W. Baker (London) and J. M. Neale (London), and is in the public domain.

CHILDREN OF DUST

Small children of dust,
Feeble and frail,
In we you must trust,
We pray you not fail.

We sing of your grace,
We help you to heal,
Your pain we replace,
With humble reveal.

My poem, has roots in lyrics from the hymn "Psalm 104," which is in the public domain.

CHILDREN'S RHYME

Little drops of water,
Little grains of sand,
Little words of love,
Sent from heaven above.

Little deeds of kindness,
Done by youthful hands,
Enrich and bless the people,
And the beauteous land.

Little prayers at bedtime,
And throughout the day,
Puts our faith in focus,
Young conviction, on display.

My poem has roots in the lyrics of "Little Things," author Mrs. T. J. Carney (1895), which is in the public domain.

Do Not Wait

Do not wait for some great deed,
To brighten the corner where you are.
Proceed unlike the centipede,
Don't slowly cast your spell afar.

A stranger stands in front of you,
From all your talent, fill his need.
Tender him a warm preview,
Give the bread of life that feeds.

My poem has roots in lyrics from the hymn "Brighten the Corner Where You Are," by Ina Duley Ogdon, which is in the public domain.

EAGERLY I SING

How eagerly I sing,
As I salute the King,
In peerless beauty He,
Dons grace eternally.

Put on Thy majesty,
And richest panoply,
In meekness and in right,
Spite wrong with wizardly might.

O flock, believe and heed,
Bring faith to him, our Lord,
Let all doubt recede,
Full fealty accord.

My poem has roots in the lyrics of "A Goodly Theme Is Mine," Tune: Fairfield (La Trobe), which is in the public domain.

Epitaph 1

A friend to many is sadly missed,
Each duty done, he rests in peace,
Dying is but going home,
Peace at last is what lives on.

Faith in My Heart

Be thou my vision of faith in my heart,
Naught all be else to me, save that thou art,
Thou my great Father, I thy true son,
Thou in me dwelling, and I with he one.

Be thou my battle shield, sword for my fight.
Be thou my dignity, thou my delight.
Riches I need not, nor man's empty praise,
Faith my inheritance, now and always.

My poem has roots in lyrics from the hymn "Be Thou My Vision," (c1700), translated by Mary E. Byrne, versified by Eleanor H. Hull, and is in the public domain.

FAITH IS MY ALL

Be thou my vision, faith in my heart,
Naught be all else to me, save that thou art,
Thou my best thought by day or by night,
Waking or sleeping, true faith is my light.

Be thou my wisdom, and thou my true word,
I ever with thee, together for good.
Peace in my dwelling, and I with thee one,
My dignity, my faith, all in unison.

Riches I need not, nor pride's empty praise,
Thou my inheritance, now and always.
Thou and thou only, first in my heart,
Soul deep my faith, my treasure thou art.

High King of heaven, my victory won,
May I reach heaven's joys, o bright heaven's sun,
Heart of my own heart, whatever befall,
Still be my vision, for faith is my all.

My poem has roots in the lyrics of "Be Thou My Vision," author Mary E. Byrne and versifier Eleanor H. Hull, which is in the public domain.

Faith, My Hope, My Light

The sunshine in my soul today,
More glorious and bright,
Than glows in any earthly sky,
Faith, my hope, my light.

The music in my soul today,
Hope and faith I bring,
All those listening can hear,
Songs of fidelity, I sing.

The music in my soul today,
For when my faith is near,
The dove of peace sings in my heart,
The flowers of grace appear.

There is gladness in my soul today,
Based on hope, on praise and love.
For tidings given to me now,
For joys foretold above.

My poem has roots in lyrics from the hymn "Sunshine in the Soul," author Eliza Edmunds Hewitt (born 1851), which is in the public domain.

Gift of Faith

Give me the gift of faith to rise,
Within my life to see,
The heavens above, how great the joys,
How bright the glories be.

Cease all mourning here below,
Don't wet the couch with tears,
Faith wrestles hard, as we do now,
With sins, and doubts, and fears.

Faith will lead us and claim our praise,
The loving life now given,
Shows us how to stand and raise,
Our face to the path to Heaven.

My poem has roots in the lyrics of "Give Me the Wings of Faith," author Isaac Watts (1709), which is in the public domain.

Grant Us Peace

Grant us peace on our homeward way,
In peace we began and will end the day.
Pause sinful thoughts and hearts from shame,
That in this house no cause to blame.

Grant us peace through the coming night,
Bring us from darkness into light,
From harm and peril, keep children free,
In light and dark, please stay with me.

Grant us peace through this earthly life,
Our balm in sorrow, our stay in strife.
When thy voice shall bid our conflict cease,
Guide us to thy perfect peace.

My poem has roots in lyrics from the work "Parting Hymn," by John Ellerton (1866), which is in the public domain.

HEAVENLY BURDEN

Who for all our burdens bear,
Who for all his people cares,
Our Lord is strong enough to save,
And ransom us from the grave.

Ye kingdoms of the earth,
Praise his matchless worth,
His triumphs in the heavens broad,
Mountains tremble at the voice of God.

Honors ascribed to God on high,
People who on his power rely,
Thine awesome glories shine,
Unending praise be thine.

My poem has roots in lyrics from the hymn "O Lord, Thou Hast Ascended," a missionary hymn (late 1800s), which is in the public domain.

Heavenly Frame

A calm and heavenly frame,
A light to shine upon the road,
That leads me to the chosen name.

Where the blessedness I knew,
When first I sought the word,
There, I found rare review.

How sweet the memory still,
Of peaceful hours, once enjoyed,
Now a hollow void, need to be filled.

Return please, sweet messenger of rest,
I repent the sins that make me mourn,
And all hope that spills from my breast.

Return, oh leap of faith, return,
My sins no more to mourn,
And please, oh faith, quell life's concerns.

My poem has roots in lyrics from the hymn "Walking With God," author William Cowper (1772), which is in the public domain.

His Command

Human pride and earthly glory,
Sword and crown betray our trust.
What with care and toil we buildeth,
Lest our towers fall to dust.

Daily doth the mighty giver,
Bounteous gifts on us bestow,
Our desire and our soul delighteth,
Pleasure leads us where we go.

Still from earth to faith eternal,
Sacrifice of praise be done.
High above all praises praising,
Yield to faith's phenomenon.

My poem has roots in lyrics from the hymn "God, My Hope on You Is Founded," written by Joachim Neander and translated by Robert Bridges (1600s), which is in the public domain.

Holy Fast and Hunger Sore

Oh love, how deep, how broad, how high,
How obedient thought should amplify,
Our daily oeuvre indeed should make,
High regard for our mortal state.

Holy fast and hunger sore,
Through our lust and penance bore,
For our temptations sharp debut,
From loving favor, we withdrew.

For we wicked souls did betray,
The gift of Eden faith had arrayed,
Until upon a cross of death,
Hope in life's form gave up his breath.

For us how deep, how high again,
For us faith went on high to reign,
Took us along with hearts sincere,
To guide, to strengthen, and to cheer.

My poem has roots in lyrics from the hymn "Oh Love, How Deep, How Broad, How High," attributed to Thomas á Kempis (1400s), and translated by Benjamin Webb (1852), which is in the public domain.

I Come

Out of my darkness, sorrow and night,
Into our friendship, gladness and light.

Out of my sickness, into my health,
Out of "my wants," into my wealth,
Out of the sin and disdain for myself,
I stop my worries, stack woes on the shelf.

Out of life's worry, into the sun,
Out of life's storms, led by your calm,
Out of distress, hearing jubilant songs,
I know now it's true, with you I belong.

Out of unrest, arrogance and pride,
Into my friendship with you I abide,
Out of myself, to dwell in real love,
Out of despair, I see raptures above.

Out of the depths of fears still untold,
Into this friendship, this sheltering fold,
My friend, your glorious face I behold,
Forever friend, my centerfold.

My poem has roots in lyrics from the hymn "Jesus, I Come," author William T. Sleeper (1887), which is in the public domain.

I Praise and Sing

Standing on the promises, I praise and sing,
Through eternal ages may his praises ring,
Glory on the highest, I will shout and sing.

Standing on promises that cannot fail,
When the storms of doubt and fear assail,
By the living work in faith, we will prevail.

Standing on the promises, I cannot fail,
Listening intently to the Spirit's call,
Knowing my savior is my all in all.

Standing on the promises, I pray and sing.

My poem has roots in lyrics from the hymn "Standing on The Promises," author Russell Kelso Carter (1886), which is in the public domain.

Join To Sing

Forevermore we'll sing,
Our praise be to our King,
Let all, with heart and voice,
Before his throne rejoice.

Lift your hearts on high,
Let praises fill the sky,
Not just faith but friend,
His love shall never end.

Praise yet our King, again,
Life shall end the strain,
On Heaven's blissful shore,
His goodness we'll adore.

My poem has roots in lyrics from the hymn "Come, Christians, Join to Sing," author Christian H. Bateman (1843), which is in the public domain.

Let Our Joys Be Known

We that love the Lord,
Let our joys be known,
Sing a song with sweet accord,
Our heart faith's metronome.

Let those who do not sing,
And do not know our surety,
Sweet children of heavenly faith,
Praise in their own community.

So, let all praise abound,
Let all eyes be dry,
The faithful march spellbound,
To a fairer world on high.

My poem has roots in the lyrics of "Come, Ye that Love the Lord," author Isaac Watts, which is in the public domain.

LIBERTY

Take my life and let it be,
There's no life sans liberty,
Take my hands so they may move,
No independence? I disapprove.

Take my feet, let them trod,
Swiftly on freedom's sod,
Take my voice and let me sing,
Liberty will be my king.

Take my silver and my gold,
Not a tyrant would I hold,
Take my moments and my days,
No tyrant will I ever praise.

Release my will and it is mine,
Independence is my shrine,
It shall be my home, my own
Liberty, life's royal throne.

My poem has roots in lyrics from the hymn "Take My Life and Let It Be," author Frances Ridley Haveryal (1647), which is in the public domain.

Lift Glories High

Let all that dwell above the sky,
In air, and earth, then raise,
Conspire to lift thy glories high,
And speak thine endless praise.

The whole creation joins as one,
To bless the sacred name,
Of Him that sits upon the throne,
And to adore the Lamb.

"Worthy, the Lamb that died," they cry,
"To be exalted thus."
"Worthy the Lamb," we then reply,
"Sacrificed for us."

He is worthy to receive,
Honor and power divine;
And blessings, more than we can give,
His grace forever mine.

My poem has roots in lyrics from the hymn "Come Let Us Join Our Cheerful Songs," by Isaac Watts (1701), which is in the public domain.

Loss and Pride

My richest gain I count but loss,
And pour contempt on all my pride,
All the vain things that charm me most,
Belie the truth, and foretell lies.

Did sorrow and love commingle down?
Did ever such love and sorrow meet?
Love so amazing, so divine,
And man? Our homage incomplete.

Were the whole realm of nature, mine,
That be a present far too small,
For love so amazing, so divine,
I'd give my soul, my life, my all.

My poem has roots in lyrics from the hymn "Crucifixion to the World by the Death of Christ," author Isaac Watts (1707), which is in the public domain.

Majesty

Ride on, ride on in majesty!
As the tribes in praise do cry.

Ride on, ride on in majesty,
In triumph now to die.

Ride on, ride on in majesty,
The winged squadrons of the sky.

Ride on, ride on in majesty,
Your last strife on earth is nigh.

Ride on, ride on in majesty,
In triumph now to die.

My curated poem has roots in lyrics from the hymn "Ride On! Ride On in Majesty!" author Henry Hart Milman (1827), which is in the public domain.

THE PRAYERFUL POET

MAKING WHOLE

Manifest in making whole,
Take weakened might,
And batterer soul,
Quelling all confusion's fright,
Manifest in making whole.

My poem has roots in lyrics from the hymn "Songs of Thankfulness and Praise," author Christopher Wordsworth (1862), which is in the public domain.

Meadows Fair

Fair are the meadows,
Flourishing in the spring,
Cloaked in fledgling flowers,
Arousing hearts to sing.

Fair is the moonlight,
Bright stars amplify,
Dazzling twilight sight,
Celestial fireflies.

My poem has roots in lyrics from the hymn "Beautiful Savior," author Joseph Augustus Seiss, which is in the public domain.

MELODIOUS SONNET

Teach me a melodious sonnet,
Sung by flaming tongues above,
Praise the ideal, I'm fixed upon it,
Built on faith's redeeming love.

There, I find my greatest treasure,
With faith and guidance, I have come,
And I hope, by thy good pleasure,
Safely to arrive at home.

Oh, to grace I am a debtor,
Daily I'm constrained to be,
Let thy goodness, like a fetter,
Bind my heart to faith, indeed.

My poem has roots in the lyrics from the hymn "Come, Thou Fount of Every Blessing," author Robert Robinson (1758) and alterer Martin Madan (1760), which is in the public domain.

Neither High nor Low

The heavens are not too high,
Our praises may thither fly.
The earth is not too low,
For peace and love to grow.

The throngs with praise must shout,
No door can keep them out.
But more than all, the heart,
Must bear the steadfast part.

The heavens are not too high,
Our thanks we'll amplify,
In voices never low,
Our gratitude will overflow.

My curated poem has roots in lyrics from the hymn "Let All the World in Every Corner Sing," author George Herbert (1619), which is in the public domain.

O, Hear Us

Oh hear us when we cry to thee,
For those in peril on the sea,
O Savior, whose almighty word,
The winds and waves submissively heard.

For those in peril on the sea,
Who walked upon the foaming deep,
From winds and waves their shelter be,
And calmly offer respite sleep.

O Holy Spirit, who did brood,
Upon the waters dark and rude,
And bid their angry tumult cease,
And exchange for wild confusion and peace.

Oh majesty of love and power.
Raise fidelity's shield in peril's hour,
From rock and tempest, to be heard,
Give O Savior, your almighty word.

My poem has roots in lyrics from the hymn "Eternal Father, Strong to Save," author William Whiting (1860), which is in the public domain.

Oblation

Vainly we offer our simple oblation,
Vainly with gifts, we would try and secure,

Richer by far, is the heart's adoration,
Dearer to assent are the prayers of the poor.

Brightest and best the sons of the morning,
Dawn on our darkness and lend us thine aid.

Star of the east, the horizon adorning,
Guide us to where our conviction is laid.

My poem has roots in lyrics from the hymn "Brightest and Best of the Sons of the Morning," author Reginald Heber (1811), which is in the public domain.

Practice of Good

Strive for redemption with the practice of good,
That as a believer you see hope understood.
Know the vilest offender who truly believes,
At that moment of faith, sees forgiveness received.

Our faith be the glory, great things to be done!
Faith holds us steady and gives us the one,
Who in this life gave atonement for sin,
And opened the gate that we may go in.

Great things he has taught us, great things to be done,
And great our rejoicing through faith's only son.
But purer and higher and greater will be,
Our wonder, our transport, when heaven we see.

My poem has roots in the lyrics from the hymn "To God Be The Glory," author Fanny Crosby (1875), which is in the public domain.

Rejoice

With heart and soul and voice,
Full hearts in gratitude we say,
Be ye near to endless bliss,
Proclamation when a heart parlays,
To fill both heart and soul with voice.
Rejoice.

My poem has roots in lyrics from the hymn "Good Christian Friends, Rejoice," author John Mason Neale, which is in the public domain.

Softly and Tenderly

Our faith is calling,
To guide our destiny,
Ever watching and waiting,
For you and for me.

Why do we tarry,
When all are pleading,
Why do we linger?
And not be free.

Time is now fleeting,
The moments are passing,
Deathbeds are coming,
For you and for me.

Oh, salvation we've been promised,
Though we have sinned,
We'll have mercy and pardon,
In our faith's origin.

My poem has roots in lyrics from the hymn "Softly and Tenderly Jesus is Calling," author Will L. Thompson (1880), which is in the public domain.

Beverly Stock

Someday

Someday the silver cord will break,
For us, no more shall we sing.
But oh, the joy when we wake,
Within the peace of eternity.

Someday my earthly house will fail,
I cannot tell how soon it will be,
But this I know, my all-in-all,
Waits for me in eternity.

If, one day the sun does fade,
Beneath the rosy-tinted west,
My life will be called, "Well done!"
And I shall enter into rest.

Until that day I'll watch and wait,
My hope confirmed, and burning bright.
When my time comes at the gate,
My faith and hope will take flight.

My poem has roots in the lyrics from the hymn "Saved by Grace," author Fanny Crosby (1891), which is in the public domain.

Stand Up

The trumpet call we must obey,
In this most glorious day,
Against those unnumbered foes,
With strength and vigor to oppose.

Stand up in faith alone,
Ye dare not trust your own.
Rely on gospel armor,
Where duty calls to danger.

The strife will not be long,
Before the next victor's song,
A crown of life shall be,
Peace and grace eternally.

My poem has roots in lyrics from the hymn "Stand Up, Stand Up for Jesus," author George Duffield (1858), which is in the public domain.

TAKE A LOOK

O soul, are you weary and troubled,
No light in the dark do you see?
There's a gleam at the end of the tunnel,
Promise of life, abundant and free.

Take a long look down life's highway,
Look full for simplicity and grace.
And strife might grow strangely dim,
Embrace this calm, peaceful place.

Fear not what cannot be,
Pledge your gratitude for what is there,
Over us sorrow has no dominion,
For more than survivors we are.

An attitude of gratitude shall not fail you,
Believe it and all will be well.
Then go to the world that is dying,
Bring calm to all infidels.

My poem has roots in the lyrics from the hymn "Turn Your Eyes Upon Jesus," author Helen Howarth Lemmel (1922), which is in the public domain.

Take Up Thy Cross

If you would my disciple be,
Take up your cross with willing heart,
And humbly follow after me.

Take up your cross, let its weight,
Not fill your spirit with alarm,
Brace your heart and brace your arm.

Take up your cross, battle danger brave,
And let your foolish heart be still,
Accepting death is victory o'er the grave.

My curated poem has roots in lyrics from the hymn "Take Up Thy Cross, the Savior Said," author Charles W. Everest (1833), which is in the public domain.

Tell The Story

I often tell my children of higher things above,
Of angels and their glory, of kindness and of love.
I tell this tale to them because I know each word is true,
Each time I look into their eyes and simply say "I love You."

Every time I tell the tale of how our love began,
Each telling seems more profound and altogether grand.
Of all my fantasies and all my golden dreams,
To conceive a child, not to be as it had seemed.

Hungering and thirsting, is my way to say it best,
To fulfill a need, a gift of love, a mothering bequest.
Not bearing you on my own, God gave me you through her,
Through loving gift, new friends, new hope, our miracles occurred.

My poem has roots in the lyrics from the hymn "Turn Your Eyes Upon Jesus," author Kate Hankey (1866) and refrain author William G. Fischer (1869), which is in the public domain.

TEMPTATIONS

Temptations are robust,
Oh bless me now my savior,
I need thee every hour,
Temptations lose their power,
When thou art nigh.

Temptations most puissant,
I need thee every hour
Come quickly and abide,
In joy or in pain.
Lest our life be in vain.

Temptations are foreboding,
I need thee every hour,
Teach me thy will,
And thy rich promises
Your grace I may fulfill.

My poem has roots in lyrics from the hymn "I Need Thee Every Hour," author Anne S. Hawkins (1872) and author-refrain Robert Lowery (1872), which is in the public domain.

Text of Faith

Blessed be the text of faith,
Vast and boundless words,
Blessed from shore to shore,
Maintains faith forevermore.

Faith's compass points to China's wake,
Africa's sons their chains shall break;
Egypt, where Thy people trod,
Shall praise faith for mankind's sake.

India's groves of palms so fair,
Shall resound with heartfelt prayer,
Ceylon's isle with joy shall sing,
Glory be to the peace faith brings.

North and South will show the way,
East and West won't delay,
Following faith will be the call,
To the highest, all in all.

My poem has roots in the lyrics from the hymn "Great Jehovah, Mighty Lord," author Fanny Crosby (1891), which is in the public domain.

Thankfulness and Praise

Songs of thankfulness and praise,
That manifested in a star.
Were sung to the sages from afar.

Manifested in making whole,
Palsied limbs and fainting soul,
Manifested in valiant fight.

Quelling all the evils might,
Manifested in gracious will,
Ever bringing good from ill.

My poem has roots in lyrics from the hymn "Songs of Thankfulness and Praise," author Christopher Wordsworth (1862), which is in the public domain.

The Day is Ended

The day given has but ended,
The darkness falls at night's behest.
All of our morning hymns ascended,
Our work fulfilled, hallowed now our rest.

As o'er each continent and island,
The dawn leads on another day,
The voice of the faithful never silent,
Nor fades the strain of praise away.

The sun, that bid us rest, is waking,
For all those 'neath the western sky,
Hour by hours fresh lips are making,
Wondrous sayings heard on high.

So be it now, the sun shall never,
Like earth's empires, pass away,
But stand and rule and grow forever,
As all life's creatures stall and stay.

My curated poem has roots in lyrics from the hymn "The Day Thou Gavest, Lord, is Ended," author John Ellerton (1870), which is in the public domain.

THE FOUNDATION

Oh, tell me of the foundation,
If faith and love are cornerstones,
That binds the faithful from every corner,
So that no one needs to pray alone?

All those in the favored city,
Dearly loving God on high,
In triumphant jubilation,
Exalting hymns to passersby.

The foundation is of a Temple
Where the call goes out today,
With all wanted loving-kindness,
Hear thy people as they pray.

Vouchsafe here are all thy servants,
Seeking wisdom not of fame,
What they gain from thee forever,
Is his blessing to retain.

My poem has roots in lyrics from the hymn "Christ is Made the Sure Foundation," author J. M. Neale (1861), which is in the public domain.

The Fountain Filled With Blood

There is a fountain filled with blood,
Drawn from Immanuel's veins,
And sinners, plunged beneath that flood,
Lose all their guilty stains.

The dying thief rejoiced to see,
That fountain in his day,
And there may I, though, vile as he,
Wash all my sins away.

Ever since by faith I saw the stream,
Thy flowing wounds supply,
Redeeming love has been my theme,
And shall be till I die.

When this poor lisping, stammering tongue,
Lies silent in the grave,
Then a nobler, sweeter song,
I'll sing thy power to save.

My poem has roots in lyrics from the hymn "Praise for the Fountain Opened," author William Cowper (1772), which is in the public domain.

THE GIFT

Whatever the gift may be,
All that I have is thine alone,
My trust, in faith, from thee.

To find a balm for woe,
To tend the lone and fatherless,
Is mine, an angel's, work below.

To faith the lost to bring,
To teach a life of peace,
My sole and faithful thing.

Though dim our faith may be,
We do believe the word,
What 'er that we do, we do it lovingly.

My poem has roots in lyrics from the hymn "We Give Thee but Thy Own," author William Walsham How (1858), which is in the public domain.

VICTORY

Harmonies of liberty,
As the rolling sea,
A new day begun,
And won is victory.

With a steady beat,
On such weary feet,
From gloomy past,
New stars are cast.

Thus far on our way,
Lest our feet stray,
Our silent tears past,
Tall shadows we cast.

My poem has roots in the lyrics from the hymn "Lift Every Voice and Sing," author James Weldon Johnson (1900), which is in the public domain.

WHAT WONDERS WROUGHT

I rest me in the thought,
Of all the wonders wrought.
The birds their carols raise,
Declare their daily praise,
Of all that shines so fair,
In beauty everywhere.
Oh, let me not forget,
If wrong oft seems so strong,
My heart should not be sad,
Look what wonders wrought.

My poem has roots in lyrics from the hymn "The Heavens Declare Thy Glory, Lord," author Isaac Watts, which is in the public domain.

WHEN I WAKE

In honesty, for this I pray,
The wrong that I have done this day,
May fidelity with my neighbor be,
Before I sleep, restored to me.

Heaven, may I be at rest in you,
Peacefully sleep the whole night through,
Refresh my faith, for your sake,
So I may serve well when I wake.

My poem has roots in the lyrics of "An Evening Hymn," author Thomas Ken (1709), which is in the public domain.

Ye Faithful

Raise the strain of triumphant gladness,
Israel has brought joy from sadness,
Jacob's sons and daughters,
Led them through the Red Sea waters.

The queen of seasons bright,
With the day of splendor,
With the royal feast of feasts,
Comes its joy to render.

Fear not the gates of death foretold,
Nor the burial tomb's dark portal,
Faithful, thou did stand, bestowing,
Peace that passes human knowing.

My poem has roots in lyrics from the hymn "Come, Ye Faithful, Raise the Strain," author St. John of Damascus and translator, J. M. Neale, which is in the public domain.

Interlude

Readers often ask me:
   "How do you read poetry?"

My answer is:
   "Aloud, whenever possible."

There are two reasons why it's important to me to read poems aloud: the spoken word can deliver two different sensory pleasures. Certainly words deliver meaning, but they deliver a sound as well. Acoustics refers to the sounds in a poem like the crackling "C" or popping "K" sounds.

Poets must understand how to manipulate the sounds with the cadence, or the meter, in poetry.

In most learning environments, reading aloud helps improve information processing skills, vocabulary and comprehension. Reading aloud targets the skills of audio learners. There is research that shows teachers who read aloud motivate students to read. This brings about comprehension, the most important goal of reading.

-Beverly Stock

Interlude

Readers often ask me:
   Why do you read poetry?

Author:
   To achieve peace of mind.

Poetry offers me an inner state of happiness that is counter to the world of external circumstances. It brings inner life in union with faith and peace regardless of the distractions a busy life offers.

Following is a reading about happiness that I find useful for inner peace:

> *"May You Have....*
> *For every storm, a rainbow,*
> *For every tear, a smile,*
> *For every care, a promise,*
> *And a blessing in each trial.*
> *For every problem life sends,*
> *A faithful friend to share,*
> *For every sigh, a sweet song*
> *And an answer for each prayer.*
>
> — Traditional Irish Blessing

Part Two

All Ye

All ye creatures of our King,
Lift up your voice and with us sing,
Thou burning sun with golden beam,
Thou silver moon with softer gleam.

Thou rushing wind that art so strong,
Ye clouds that sail in heaven along,
Thou rising morn, in praise rejoice,
Ye lights of evening, find a voice.

Thou flowing water, pure and clear,
Make music so the faithful hear,
Thou fire so masterful and bright,
That givest man both warmth and light.

And all ye men of tender heart,
Forgiving others, take your part,
Ye who long pain and sorrow bear,
Praise faith and in it cast your care.

Let all things their faith does bless,
And worship in gentle humbleness.

My poem has roots in the lyrics of the hymn, "All Creatures of Our God and King," author St. Francis of Assisi (1225), and paraphraser William H. Draper, which is in the public domain.

ARISE

River and mountain spring,
Valley and lowland, sing,
Sing to the listening earth,
Hope of a world's new birth.

Lands of the East, arise,
Greet faith with joyous eyes.
Shores of the utmost West,
Welcome the blessed guest.

Shout, as you journey home,
Lo, from the North they come,
All in faith shall find their rest,
In faith the universe is blest.

My poem has roots in the lyrics of "Hills of the North," author Charles E. Oakley, which is in the public domain.

ASSURANCE

Heartfelt assurance,
A vow, this be mine,
Perfect submission,
For not to unwind.

This be my story,
This be my rhyme,
Watching and waiting,
For rapture divine.

My poem has roots in lyrics from the hymn "Blessed Assurance," by Fanny Crosby, which is in the public domain.

AWAKE!

Spring up! Awake! Salute the morn,
For on this day the world was born,
The angels chanted from above,
Sweet sentiments of faith and of love.

To watchful shepherds it was told,
Who heard the angelic voice: "Behold,
I bring good news of the Savior's birth,
To all the faithful on the earth."

When he spoke, the celestial choir,
In new and joyful hymns conspired,
The praises of faith they sang,
Heaven's whole orb with alleluias rang.

Oh, may we ponder in our mind,
Faith's hand in bonding all mankind,
Tread the steps, assisted by grace,
Till our imperfect state, faith does replace.

Then may we hope angelic throngs among,
To sing, redeemed, a triumphal song,
Saved by faith's love, incessant we shall sing,
Eternal praise that faith in heaven brings.

My poem has roots in the lyrics of "Christians, Awake," author John Byrom (1749), which is in the public domain.

BELOW THE SKIES

For life we know below the skies,
Our Creator's gift we'll always prize,
And may our Redeemer's name be sung,
By every man in every tongue.

Eternal truth attends Thy Word,
Eternal as your mercies, Lord.
Our praise we'll sing from shore to shore,
Till suns shall rise and set no more.

My poem has roots in lyrics from the hymn "From All that Dwell Below the Skies," author Issac Watts (1719), which is in the public domain.

BEST GIFT DIVINE

For the wonder of each hour,
Hill and vale and tree and flower,
For the wonder of each night,
Sun and moon and stars so bright.

For the joy of human love,
Friends on earth and friends above,
Brother, sister, parent, child,
For all thoughts, kind and mild.

For yourself, best gift divine,
Agent of faith's grand design,
To the world so freely given,
Peace on earth and joy in heaven.

My poem has roots in lyrics from the hymn "For The Beauty of the Earth," author Folliott Sandford Pierpoint (1864), which is in the public domain.

BLESSINGS

When in life's billows you are tossed,
When you believe all might be lost,
Count your blessings one by one,
You'll be surprised by all you've done.

When heavy with the weight of care,
Feeling strife too hard to bear.
Count your honors one by one,
Realize all the oeuvre you've done.

Never envy others, hands full of gold,
Value integrity, honesty, the new and old.
Count things earned, you cannot buy,
With milestones met, life's gratified.

My poem has roots in lyrics from the hymn "Count Your Blessings," author John Oatman (1897), which is in the public domain.

BEVERLY STOCK

BRIGHT AND BEAUTIFUL

Things are bright and beautiful,
Creatures great and small,
Each little flower that opens,
Comes to faith's great call.

The purple-headed mountain,
The river running by,
The bright sun in the winter,
That glows up the sky.

Each cold wind in the winter,
Each pleasant summer sun,
Ripe fruits in all our gardens,
He made them, every one.

With eyes he gave to see them,
And lips so we might tell,
How great is faith's great majesty,
Which has made all these things well.

My poem has roots in lyrics from the hymn "All Things Bright and Beautiful," author Cecil Frances Alexander (1848), which is in the public domain.

Church of My Childhood

No place so dear to my childhood,
As the church in the valley by the wildwood.
No lovelier spot in the dale,
As my childhood church in the vale.

When day fades away into night,
I would fain from this spot of my childhood.
From the church in the valley by the wildwood,
And wing my way to mansions of light.

My poem has roots in lyrics from the hymn "The Little Brown Church," author William S. Pitts, which is in the public domain.

Do Our Best

Life's dark trials in every hand,
Holding them we cannot stand,
All the ways that good would lead,
Anguish tries to take command.

But we persevere with gladness,
And we'll follow till we die,
Knowing what lies before us,
In our famila honeycomb.

By and by when morning comes,
And all kin are gathered home,
We will muster strength among us,
In our famila honeycomb.

If our cherished plans do fail us,
Disappointment is our veil,
Lead us not into the darkness,
Deny the thought that we might fail.

All temptations, hidden snares,
Often take us unaware,
And our hearts are made to bleed,
If, at first, we do not succeed.

May we not question why the test
May we simply try to do our best.

My poem has roots in lyrics from the hymn "We'll Understand it Better By And By," Dorothy F. Gurney (1883), which is in the public domain..

Eternal Gates of Mercy

When time was yet unknown,
Love and mercy lived alone.
Celestial creation then did bless
Us and shared consonance.

Most ancient of all mysteries,
Have mercy, now on me.
May my life's earned narratives,
Open your gates of mercy.

My poem has roots in lyrics from the hymn "Have Mercy on Us, God Most High," by F. W. Faber (1849), and is in the public domain.

Eternal Love and Life

All human thought transcending,
Prayer before thy throne,
A love which knows no ending,
Sacred vow dost join in one.

Be thou their full assurance
Of charity and faith,
Of quiet brave endurance,
That fears no pain or death.

Joy which brightens earthly sorrow,
Peace which calms all earthly strife,
Vision of the glorious morrow,
Reveal eternal love and life.

My poem has roots in lyrics from the hymn "O Perfect Love, All Human Thought Transcending" by Dorothy F. Gurney (1883), which is in the public domain.

FAITH'S HAND

Whatever I do, wherever I be,
Still 'tis faith's hand that leadeth me.
By waters calm or troubled sea,
'Tis my faith that leadeth me.

I would clasp faith's hand in mine,
Not ever murmur or repine,
Even death's cold wave I'll not flee,
Since faith's hand doth leadeth me.

My poem has roots in lyrics from the hymn "He Leadeth Me," author Joseph H. Gilmore (1862), which is in the public domain.

Find a Voice

Past rising morn, in praise rejoice,
Ye souls of evening, find a voice,
Thou flowing water, pure and clear,
Make music, faithful yearn to hear.

All ye men of tender heart,
Forgiving others, take your part,
Ye who long pain and sorrow bear,
Know faith, in it cast your care.

Let all things the Creator doth bless,
And worship them in humbleness
Praise the Father, praise the Son,
And the Spirit, three in one.

Let praise and love, in faith you bring,
Lift up your voice, with us sing.

My poem has roots in lyrics from the hymn "All Creatures of Our God and King," author St. Francis of Assisi (1225), and originally paraphrased by William H. Draper, which is in the public domain.

Funeral Thought

I think I shall converse a while,
And hold at bay, my death,
Resisting gasping mortal lies,
And not pant away my breath.

My quivering lip drops slowly down,
Words uttered? Just a few,
Soon, speechless with a lowly groan,
I'll bid the world adieu.

I know my soul shall never die,
As my bones turn into clay.
My mind races to the skies,
Seeing downcast memories parlay.

Oh, must my body faint and die,
My soul then be removed?
I need faith's guardian angel high,
To escort me home, improved.

Now, in peace I place my human hand,
But naked is the soul, in you I trust,
I wait serene for thy command,
To release my oeuvre to dust.

My poem has roots in lyrics from the hymn "Stoop Down, My Thoughts, That Use to Rise," author Isaac Watts, which is in the public domain.

Grief and Sadness

What can end the pain and stain?
Quiet all my grief and sadness,
What can make me whole again?
Quenching all my grief and sadness.

Life, so precious is the flow,
Handled freely to and fro,
No better joy do I know,
Silencing my grief and sadness.

For my pardon, this I see,
A choice of paths that must be,
For my cleansing, this my plea,
Save me from my grief and sadness.

Nothing can for death atone,
Fate has spoken, it's mine alone,
Naught of cure that I have done,
Again, in my grief and sadness.

This is all my hope and peace,
My reprieve bought and complete,
I'm ready in my righteousness,
Leaving all my grief and sadness.

My poem has roots in lyrics from the hymn "Nothing But the Blood of Jesus," author Robert Lowry (1876), which is in the public domain.

GUIDANCE

I am just a pilgrim in this barren land.
Hope consume me, lead me by the hand.
Lead me all my journey, yield.
Strong deliver, strength, and shield.
Bid my anxious fears subside.
In hope and strength I will abide.

My poem has roots in lyrics from the hymn "Guide Me, O My Great Jehovah," author William Williams (1745), which is in the public domain.

Hope and Help

HELP,
In ages past.

HOPE,
For years to come.

SHELTER,
From the stormy blast,

SAFE,
In our eternal home.

SAINTS,
Have dwelt secure.

SUFFICIENT,
Is your arms alone.

FAITH,
In our defense is sure.

TOGETHER,
For years to come.

BEFORE,
The hills in order stood,

EARTH,
Received her frame.

EVERLASTING
Is our God.

ENDLESS,
Years the same.

GOD,
Our help in ages past,

BE
Our guard while troubles last.

My poem has roots in lyrics from the hymn "O God, Our Help in Ages Past," author Isaac Watts (1719), which is in the public domain.

Beverly Stock

How Can It Be?

Tell me how that I should gain,
From causes that bring others pain?

How can it be that ill pursues,
The worst in us and then is used?

Instead, explore the elite design,
Of what we find in love divine.

So free, so infinite life's grace,
For those caught in the mortal race.

Tis love, you see, immense and free,
That urges the best of grace from me.

My poem has roots in lyrics from the hymn "And Can It Be, That I Should Gain," author Charles Wesley (1738), which is in the public domain.

Human Ending

Face to face with human ending,
Face to face - what will it be?
When in final peace I enter,
A final rest just for me.

Only faintly can I feel it,
With the darkened veil between,
I feel the blessed day is coming,
New beginning to be seen.

To rejoice in faithful presence,
When are gone all grief and pain.
When the crooked ways are straightened,
And the dark does not remain.

Great rejoicing in faithful presence,
Face to face - to see and know,
Face to face with hope and kindness,
In the everlasting glow.

My poem has roots in lyrics from the hymn "Face to Face with Christ My Savior," author Carrie Ellis Brech (1898), which is in the public domain.

I Surrender

How humbly I surrender,
Faith in you I freely give,
Your wisdom I will ever treasure,
And your gracious presence lived.

How humbly, I surrender,
Humbly at your feet I bow,
Worldly matter all forsaken,
Teaching goodness, knowing how.

How humbly I surrender,
I gave my children's minds to thee,
To fill with love and thus empower,
Their goodness your reflection be.

My poem has roots in lyrics from the hymn "I Surrender All," author Rebecca A. Pollard, which is in the public domain.

IN THE DARKNESS

Speak of peace,
To those in darkness,
Heavy under sorrow's load.
Grief is raw repentance,
If when pride we often hoard.

Make straight what was crooked,
Make the rough places plain,
Heavy under sorrow's load.
In our hearts let all be humble,
Fail not under sorrow's strain.

My poem has roots in lyrics from the hymn "Comfort, Comfort, Now My People," author Johann Olearius (1671), and translator Catherine Winkworth, which is in the public domain.

Just Beyond The River

Trust in the cross,
Be my glory forever,
Till my ransomed soul finds,
Rest beyond the river.

There the bright and morning start,
Shed his beams around me.
Help me walk from day to day,
With its shadow o'er me.

I'll watch and wait, trusting ever,
On the strand, just beyond the river.

My poem has roots in lyrics from the hymn "Near the Cross," author Fanny Crosby (1869), which is in the public domain..

LOST IN THE DARKNESS

The whole world was lost in the darkness,
The light of the world was gone,
Sunshine at noonday denied its place,
The light of the world was gone.

I yearned for the light shining so free,
Often the light had dawned upon me,
But now, I feel blind, alas cannot see,
The light of the world is gone.

No darkness have we if we have hope,
Hope breaks free, eager to abide,
Hope strengthens valor, posture, and desire,
Hope sees our lot with much clearer eyes.

Ye dwellers in darkness with sin-blinded eyes,
No need of a compass we're told,
Hope is thy valor, savior and strength,
For us all, the young and the old.

My poem has roots in the lyrics from the hymn "The Light of the Work is Jesus," author P. P. Bliss (1875), which is in the public domain.

LOVE DIVINE

Awake, awake to love divine,
And let its warmth upon us shine.

Then cleansed be every life from sin,
Make straight the way for hope within.

Stretch forth your love, our health restore,
Make seize and fall no more.

May graciousness upon us shine,
And fill us all with love divine.

My poem has roots in lyrics from the hymn "On Jordan's Bank the Baptist's Cry," author Charles Coffin (1676-1749) and translated by John Chandler (1837), which is in the public domain.

Lowly Bed

Once, a mother laid her baby,
In a lowly cattle-shed,
Mary, as the mother, smiled,
Making his make-shift bed.

His journey was from heaven,
His purpose to be Lord of all,
Being sheltered in a stable,
His make-shift bed, a stall.

He flourished in his childhood,
He did honor and obey,
His Mother always smiling,
In whose gentle arms he stayed.

Fear not, we all shall see him,
Thru his own redeeming love,
For that little baby,
Is our Lord in heaven above.

We'll see him not in the stable,
With cattle standing by,
He will greet us in heaven,
Set at God's right hand on high.

My poem has roots in lyrics from the hymn "Once in Royal David's City," author Cecil Frances Alexander (1848), which is in the public domain.

Mercy Broken

Bread of the world in mercy broken,
Wine of the soul in mercy shed,
By whom the words of life were spoken,
In whose death our sins are dead.

Look in the heart by sorrow broken,
See the tears by sinners shed,
And be the symbol and the token,
That by thy grace our souls are fed.

Then by thy hand let hope prevail,
Let love encircle in winsome veil,
Your hope for us is unmatched,
Us to our destiny, you dispatch.

My poem has roots in lyrics from the hymn "Bread of the World, in Mercy Broken," author Reginald Heber (1827), which is in the public domain.

MERCY CROWNED

On faith, I have now sworn,
I on this oath depend,
I shall on eagle wings unborn,
To faith's command ascend.

The heavenly land we'll see,
With peace and plenty blest,
A land of sacred liberty,
And endless, peaceful rest.

There milk and honey flow,
And oil and wine abound,
The trees of life forever grow,
And mercy duly crowned.

My poem has roots in lyrics from the hymn "The God of Abraham Praise," attributed to Daniel ben Judah and paraphraser Thomas Olivers (1770), which is in the public domain.

Mercy's Child

I think of my contentment daily,
I think in peace all the day long.
I sing, for I cannot be silent,
Faithfulness is my song.

Redeemed, and no longer restless,
No language can my rapture tell.
I know that the light of presence,
With me doth continually dwell.

Redeemed, now to proclaim it,
Redeemed from the curse of man.
Redeemed through faithful mercy,
Mercy's child, I forever am.

My poem has roots in lyrics from the hymn "Redeemed, How I Love to Proclaim It!," author Fanny Crosby (1882), which is in the public domain.

MIGHTY GATES

Lift up your heads at the mighty gates,
And there, the gift of faith awaits,
Cause for true belief is here,
The saving of mankind is near.

Open the portals of your heart
Ready a place, set apart,
From earthly use, for faith's employ
Adorned with prayer and love and joy.

Happiness with us will abide,
Our hearts to faith we open wide,
Let us its inner presence feel.
All peace and love in us reveal.

My poem has roots in the lyrics from the hymn "Lift Up Your Heads, Ye Mighty Gates," author Georg Weissel (1642) and translator Catherine Winkworth, which is in the public domain.

Mom

There is a name I long to hear,
Oh, so many sing its worth.
It sounds like music to my ear,
The very kindest name on earth.

It tells me of unbridled love.
A tribute to my ancestry.
It speaks of bonds from high above,
A name, part of my pedigree.

I said this name in childhood,
Perhaps 1,000 times per day.
Having my own child, that I could-
My loving everyday bouquet.

It tells of one with loving heart,
And gentle touch, a calming balm.
With whom in my life I did start,
My very own, my dearest Mom.

My poem has roots in lyrics from the hymn "Oh, How I Love Jesus," author Frederic Whitfield, which is in the public domain.

This poem was first published by the Society of Classical Poets https://classicalpoets.org/2019/05/12/poetry-for-mothers-day-mom-by-beverly-stock/

My Compass

My compass shows no east or west,
Indeed, no south or north,
But all directions bound by love
Throughout the whole wide earth.

People in lands everywhere,
Their high communion find;
Humanity their golden cord,
Close binding humankind.

Join hands, disciples of this world,
Who'er your kind might be,
Who live in peace and harmony,
Are surely kin to me.

Our lives combine both east and west,
We meet at south and north,
Our souls be blessed together now,
Throughout this whole wide earth.

My curated poem has roots in lyrics from the hymn "In Christ There is No East or West," author John Oxenham (1908), which is in the public domain.

My Vision

Through my vision,
Deep in my heart,
Naught be all else,
I must this impart.

Riches I need not,
Nor man's empty praise,
Honesty my inheritance,
Now and always.

When my victory won,
On path all my own,
I'll know heaven's joy,
In radiant sun shown.

My poem has roots in lyrics from the hymn "Be Through My Vision," author Mary E. Byrne (1905), which is in the public domain.

Mysterious Way

In most mysterious ways,
We ride inside the storm.
Deep in undetermined depths,
We rise, a resolution formed.

Fresh courage often takes,
Valor we so much dread.
To break the strife we make,
Our doubts, long webs, unthread.

My poem has roots in lyrics from the hymn "God Moves in a Mysterious Way," author William Cowper (1774), which is in the public domain.

On the Wings of the Storm

Dark is the path on the wings of the storm,
Circling in wrath, deep thunderclouds form,
Water streams down the hills, descends to the plains,
Sweetly distills in the earth, filled and then tamed.

We'll tell of this night and sing of this place,
With darkness surrounding this canopied space,
We breathe in the air, in the moonlight we stand,
In harmony, faith and hope, all in hand.

Brave souls of dust, feeble and frail,
In faith we find trust, in faith we prevail,
Mercies how tender, how firm to the end,
Our author, curator, hero and friend.

My poem has roots in lyrics from the hymn "O Worship the King all Glorious Above," author Robert Grant (1883), which is in the public domain.

One Holy Passion

One holy passion that calls my name,
My heart an altar, and your love the flame.
Teach me the struggles of the soul to bear,
Teach me the patience of unceasing prayer.

Oh, let me seek you and oh, let me find.
Love you with all my heart, strength and mind.
Take the dimness of my soul away,
No sudden rending of the veil of clay.

My poem has roots in lyrics from the hymn "Spirit of God, Descend Upon My Heart," author George Croly (1854), which is in the public domain.

Praise the Name

Early in the morning,
Our song shall rise to thee.

Casting down golden crowns,
Into the glassy sea.

Though the eye of sinful man,
Thy glory may not see,

All thy works shall praise thy name,
In earth and sky and sea.

My poem has roots in lyrics from the hymn "Holy, Holy, Holy! Lord God Almighty!," author Reginald Heber (1862), which is in the public domain.

Straight Race

Lay hold on life, and it shall be,
The joy and crown eternally.
Run straight the race through life's good grace,
And with thine eyes and soul embrace.

Cast care aside; in peace abide,
Trust and mercy, be your guide.
Faint not, nor fear, faith is ever near,
All knowing is our overseer.

My poem has roots in lyrics from the hymn "Fight the Good Fight," author John S. B. Monsell (1863), which is in the public domain.

STRENGTH OF FAITH

May the strength of faith,
Live in me, this I pray,
By intent and power guiding,
All I do and all I say.

May the strength of faith dwell richly,
In my heart from hour to hour,
So that all may see I triumph,
That I may be empowered.

May I run the race before me,
Strong and brave to face my foe,
My belief strong and free,
Holding steadfast as I go.

My poem has roots in lyrics from the hymn "May the Mind of Christ, My Savior," author Kate B. Wilkinson (1925), which is in the public domain.

STRENGTH WITHIN

Trust in faith to guide you,
Listen to the heartfelt hymns,
You'll find faith just there inside you,
Hope and strength deep within.

Be thy still, await faith's pleasure
Cheerful hope and heart content,
Faith fills your needs to fullest measure,
With the trust and promise love has sent.

Sing and pray, your ways unswerving,
Faith does not forsake the need,
Trust the word, though undeserving,
Offer service faithfully.

My poem has roots in lyrics from the hymn "If Thou but Suffer God to Guide Thee," author Georg Neumark (1641) and translation by Catherine Winkworth (1863), which is in the public domain.

Striving

Our striving would be losing,
But for Man of God's own choosing,
A bulwark never failing,
Of mortal ills prevailing.
Does seek to cure our woe,
Against all omnipotent foes,
His craft and power great,
True keeper of our fate.

My poem has roots in lyrics from the hymn "A Mighty Fortress," author Martin Luther (1529) and translator Frederick H. Hedge (1852), which is in the public domain.

The Joy of The Meek

O joy of all the meek,
With sweetness fills the breast,
How good to those who seek,
Thy presence for their rest.

The hope of every contrite heart,
O joy of all the meek,
To those that fail, how kind thou art,
How good to those who seek.

But what to those who find,
Not tongue nor pen can show,
The joy of faith, what it is,
His followers truly know.

Yes, Jesus, our only joy be thou,
As though our prize will be,
Jesus, be thou our glory now,
Through all eternity.

My poem has roots in lyrics from the hymn "Jesus, the Very Thought of Thee," attributed to Bernard of Claorvaux and translator Edward Caswall, which is in the public domain.

Beverly Stock

THE POET

Walk with the poet, hear songs in his words,
What glorious verse he shares on our way.
As he speaks his rhyme, he abides us be still,
To experience hypnotic rhyme, we heed and obey.

Trust and take heed, for there's no other way,
Not a shadow does rise, not a cloud in the skies,
His utterance of true message, his glib repartee,
As to his truth and testimony, I identify.

Tales of grief, or of cost, or of love's labor lost
Or the favor bestowed if we're blest and we trust.
For the favor he shows and the joy he bestows,
Hearing his rapture aloud, an invitation august.

My poem has roots in lyrics from the hymn "Trust and Obey," author John H. Sammis (1887), which is in the public domain.

THE STORY OF YOU

Tell me the story of you.
Write on my heart every word.
Tell me the parts most precious.
Truest that's ever been told.

Tell me how bands of nurses,
Sang as they welcomed your birth,
Helping your Mother survive it,
Praising her strength and her worth.

Tell me the story of you.
Tell of the days that are past,
How you became one so tempted,
How you triumphed at last.

Tell me of years of your labor.
Tell all the sorrows you bore,
How you emerged from conflict,
More focused and secure than before.

Tell of the plot where you laid her,
Your Mother's life ending in pain,
Tell of the sense when you're by her,
Headstone in sun and in rain.

It's a love story so tender,
Clearer than I ever did see.
Stay, and I'll weep while you whisper,
Of the friendship she had with thee.

My poem has roots in the lyrics from the hymn "Tell Me the Story of Jesus," author Fanny Crosby (1880), which is in the public domain.

The Test

What think you of faith is the test,
Test both your state and your scheme,
You cannot think right of the rest,
Unless you hold faith most supreme.

Some call Him a creature to be,
A man or an angel at most,
Sure they have not feelings like me,
Nor know themselves wretched, and lost.

Some call Him a Savior in word,
But mix their own works with his plan,
And hope His help will afford,
When they have done all that they can.

Some style Him the pearl of great price,
And say He's the fountain of hope,
Yet feed upon folly and vice,
And cleave to faith then elope.

If asked what of faith I think,
Although my best thoughts are poor,
I say faith's my meat and my drink,
My life and my strength at my core.

My poem has roots in the lyrics from the hymn "What Think Ye of Christ, is the Test," author John Newton (1750), which is in the public domain.

THE VOICE OF JESUS

When my soul was whole but weary,
I heard the voice of Jesus say,
"Come unto me and rest
Your head upon my breast."

I came to Jesus as I was,
Weary, worn and sad,
Joined him in a resting place,
And he then made me glad.

"Behold, I freely give,
The living water, thirsty one."
I came to Jesus and I drank,
Of the life giving stream.

I looked to Jesus and I found
In him my star, my sun,
And in that light of life I'll walk,
'Til traveling days are done.

My poem has roots in lyrics from the hymn "I Heard the Voice of Jesus Say," author Horatius Bohar (1846), which is in the public domain.

This Is The Time

Good people, no more delay.
Come now, enter at his call,
Today's the Lord's acceptance day,
To live with him who died for all.

If you believe his record true,
Enjoy the feast, be saved from sin,
Then dine with him as he with you.
You are invited, please come in.

Both good and evil in me do,
Delayed, depressed by things undone,
My weak days come in pairs of two,
Guide me, whose dreams and deeds are one.

My poem has roots in lyrics from the hymn "Come, Sinners to the Gospel Feast," author Charles Wesley (1747), which is in the public domain.

Thou Savior Dear

Thou Savior dear,
If thou be near,
No cloud will arise
To shroud you from my eyes.

The dews of kindly sleep,
My eyelids gently steep,
To think, how sweet to rest,
On my Savior's breast.

With me from morn till eve,
So fully will I live,
When night is nigh, without
Thee I dare not die.

Bless me when I wake,
Through the world my way I take,
Stay with me till in thy love,
I lose myself in heaven above.

My poem has roots in lyrics from the hymn "Sun of My Soul, Thou Savior Dear," author John Keble (1820), which is in the public domain.

Thy Church

Thy Church,
Her walls before thee stand,
And graven on thy hand.

For her my prayers ascend,
'Til toils and cares shall end.

I praise her heavenly ways,
Her hymns of love and praise.

Beyond my highest joy,
Her sweet communion vows.

Our Savior and our King,
Will great deliverance bring.

Thy Church,
Sure as thy truth shall last,
And yield success for every test.

My poem has roots in lyrics from the hymn "I Love Thy Kingdom, Lord," alterer Timothy Dwight (1800), which is in the public domain.

The Prayerful Poet

Triumph Song

Hope and peace we do adore you,
Filled with glory, filled with love,
Hearts unfold like flowers before you,
Heaven's rays shine from above.

All the work of joy surrounds you,
Solemnly fills unbroken praise,
Chanting bird and flowing fountain,
Promising hope eternally.

Mortals are the mighty chorus,
Victors in the midst of strife,
Faith and love are reigning o'er us,
In the triumph song of life.

My poem has roots in lyrics from the hymn "Joyful, Joyful, We Adore Thee," author Henry Van Dyke (1907), which is in the public domain.

Trust And Obey

In the light of the word,
What glory faith sheds on our way,
While we do good our will,
We are still, we trust and obey.

Not a burden we bear,
Not a sorrow we share,
Not a grief or a loss,
If we trust and obey.

Alas, we can't prove,
The delights of this love,
Until the end where we lay,
Grateful to trust and obey.

My poem has roots in lyrics from the hymn "Trust and Obey," author John H. Sammis (1887), which is in the public domain.

Truth Unchanged

Joy of loving hearts,
The fount of life,
Thou light of men,
From fullest bliss,
That earth imparts,
We turn to thee again.

The truth unchanged,
Has ever stood,
Thou save those,
That on thee call,
To them that seek,
We turn to thee again.

O living bread,
Long to feast,
Upon thee still,
The fountain-head,
And thirst our souls,
From thee to fill.

My poem has roots in lyrics from the hymn "Jesu, Thou Joy of Loving Hearts," translator Ray Palmer (1858) and author Bernard of Clairvaux (c1160), which is in the public domain.

WHERE O DEATH?

Where o death is thy sting?
Punctured by a sharpened fang,
That a mighty cobra brings,
Poison to my heart and brain?

Fight the fight, the battle won,
I'll choose not battle but to rise,
Instead of death I'll cross above,
Ignore temptation, no compromise.

Where o death is thy sting?
Not now death, I'm worshiping.

My poem has roots in the lyrics from the hymn "O Death, Where Is Thy Sting," author Steven Popovich (2016), composed by John Darwall (1750), which is in the public domain.

WONDERS

The wonders of your hand,
Proclaim in every land,
Repeats from hour to hour,
Day unto day the power.

The sun does chant your praise,
With gentle anthem raised,
Sun of royal splendor and,
Moonbeams soft and hazed.

The stars with solemn voices,
Resound your praises still,
Each thought indeed, all choices,
Reflect my faith and will.

My poem has roots in lyrics from the hymn "The Heavens Declare Your Glory," author Isaac Watts (1700), which is in the public domain.

Worship Above

Our shield and defender,
In ancient of days,
Pavilioned in splendor,
And girded with praise.

Do tell of his might,
Sing of his grace,
Whose robe is the light,
In a canopied space.

His bountiful care,
What tongue can recite,
It breathes in the air,
It shines in the light.

Oh, measureless might,
Unchangeable love,
Whom angels delight,
To worship above.

My poem has roots in lyrics from the hymn "O, Worship the King All Glorious Above," author Robert Grant (1833), which is in the public domain.

Afterword

The beauty of found text is that it...

Can be found in many larger poems, by well-known poets, most significantly *Ezra Pound*. His *Cantos* includes letters written by presidents and popes, as well as an array of official documents from governments and banks. *The Waste Land*, by **T. S. Eliot** uses many different texts, including Wagnerian opera, Shakespearian theater, and Greek mythology. Other poets who combined found elements with their poetry are *William Carlos Williams, Charles Olson,* and *Louis Zukofsky.*

Find more information at wikipedia.org/wiki/Found_poetry

Acknowledgements

Grateful acknowledgement to **Sandra Lesh**, without whom the author would still be searching in her Google drive for the correct file. Also, thanks to **Sandra** for her sound editing advice, for careful editing of The Prayerful Poet's Back Matter, for managing the author's website, and for years of professional friendship. To family and friends thanks for reading poems in-progress and offering honest critique and all of that unbridled encouragement. To Elm Hill and its professional staff, my everlasting gratitude.

Conclusion

By fusing *Found Poetry* with original verse, The Prayerful Poet imparts a new spirit and refreshed meaning to the words in original hymnal lyrics, while maintaining their traditional value and reverence.

Appendix

These sources were used in my historical research and to confirm title, authorship, and copyright status of all poems included in The Prayerful Poet. Many provided inspiration as well. They are as follows:

Hymnary.Org
https://hymnary.org/
An online hymn and worship music database for worship leaders, hymnologists and amateur hymn lovers alike. I used their database to research hymns by title, tune, meter, scripture reference and copyright status.

The Cyber Hymnal™
(www.hymntime.com/tch)
Is a website established in 1966 by Dick Adams. It has over 10,000 Christian hymns from many denominations and languages. It provides lyrics, sheet music, audio, pictures, biographies, and history. It is a worship and educational resource that is provided as a public service.

The Book of Common Prayer
(www.episcopalchurch.org›files›book_of_common_prayer)
The Hymnal: A Reading History, by Christopher N. Phillips
"–Every hymn begins as a poem. Once it exists as a poem, it can go in quest of accompanying music. If the quest is successful, the poem becomes a hymn in addition to a poem."

The Public Domain Project
https://www.pond5.com/free

Hymns as Poems: What Do They Mean ...
https://blog.cph.org/worship/author/marie-greenway
"Poetry is a wonderfully musical type of literature."

Biographies of my favorite authors included:

Fanny Crosby, 1820-1925. Is one of the most prolific hymnists in history, wrote over 8,000 hymns and gospel songs. Prolific in secular poems, as well.
https://hymnary.org/person/Crosby_Fanny?tab=texts

Isaac Watts, 1674-1748. The number of Isaac Watts' publications is very large. His collected works, first published in 1720, embrace sermons, treatises, poems and hymns. His hymns first appeared in July, 1707.
https://hymnary.org/person/Watts_Isaac

William Cowper, 1731-1800, (pronounced Cooper.) Cowper is regarded as one of the best early Romantic poets. To biographers he is also known as "mad Cowper." His literary talents produced some of the finest English hymn texts, but his chronic depression accounts for the somber tone of many of those texts.
https://hymnary.org/person/Cowper_W

Catalogue Copy

The Prayerful Poet is the first collection of verse from American poet Beverly Stock. Brimming with joy, wonder, and tenderness, this stirring volume takes inspiration from traditional Christian hymns and classic spiritual works.

Each poem combines Beverly's poetic adaptations with the time-honored hymnal lyrics, and finds fresh meaning in traditional songs of praise. A mixture of grand voices and elegiac laments, *The Prayerful Poet* engages readers with its hopeful perspective, and is a perfect read for anyone who finds beauty in the divine.

CPSIA information can be obtained
at www.ICGtesting.com
Printed in the USA
LVHW012353220520
656244LV00012B/55

9 781400 330805